What's in this book

This book belongs to

_____

暑假来了！
The summer holidays are here!

学习内容 Contents

沟通 Communication

说说休闲活动
Talk about leisure activities

生词 New words

★ 带	to bring
★ 床	bed
★ 网球	tennis, tennis ball
★ 河	river
★ 先	first
★ 骑马	to ride a horse
★ 然后	then, next
★ 回家	to go home
暑假	summer holidays
捉	to catch
房间	room
睡觉	to sleep
希望	to hope

背景介绍：
伊森、艾文的爷爷奶奶住在郊外。浩浩和两兄弟在他们爷爷奶奶的家门口玩。

句式 Sentence patterns

第三天，他们先去骑马，然后去爬山。

The third day, they went horse riding first, and then they went climbing.

文化 Cultures

中国的传统游戏
Traditional Chinese games

跨学科学习 Project

了解电影放映原理，并制作一本手翻书
Learn how a film works and make a flip book

Get ready

1 What did you do during the last summer holidays?

2 What do you want to do for the next summer holidays?

3 Where do you think Hao Hao is?

Summer holidays 1 July

shǔ jià
暑假

dài
带

故事大意：
暑假来了，浩浩跟着伊森、艾文来到他们的爷爷奶奶家，度过了愉快的几天。

参考问题和答案：
1 Are the children on holiday? (Yes, they are having their summer holidays.)
2 Where do Ethan and Ivan take Hao Hao? (They take him to their grandparents' home.)

暑假来了，伊森和艾文带浩浩去他们的爷爷奶奶家里玩。

chuáng
床

wǎng qiú
网球

参考问题和答案：
1 What is Hao Hao doing? (He is still in bed.)
2 What does Ivan ask him to do? (He asks Hao Hao to play tennis with him.)

"浩浩，别躺在床上了，起来打网球吧！"第二天早上，艾文说。

hé
河

zhuō
捉

参考问题和答案：

1 Where does Ethan and Ivan's grandpa take the boys? (He takes them to the river.)

2 What are they doing there? (They are fishing.)

下午，爷爷带着他们去河里捉鱼。
浩浩捉了一条大鱼。

shuì jiào
睡觉

fáng jiān
房间

参考问题和答案：
1 Where are the boys? (They are in the bedroom.)
2 Are Ethan and Hao Hao playing games? (No, they are going to bed.)

晚上，他们回到房间，伊森说："赶快睡觉吧。明天的活动更好玩。"

xiān
先

qí mǎ
骑马

我们用"先"和"然后"来表示事情发生的顺序。发生在前边的事情用"先"，在一件事情之后接着发生的事情用"然后"。

rán hòu
然后

参考问题和答案：

1 What do Ethan and Ivan's grandparents and the boys do first? (They go horse riding first.)
2 What do they do next? (They climb a hill next.)

第三天，他们先去骑马，然后去爬山。浩浩玩得很开心。

参考问题和答案：

1 Where are the boys going? (They are going home.)
2 Why is Hao Hao crossing his fingers? (Because he wishes to come back here next summer holiday. Crossing one's fingers is a sign of hoping for good luck.)

离开的时候，浩浩说："真不想回家，希望明年暑假能再来！"

Let's think

提醒学生先将故事中出现过的活动圈出，再进行排序。

1 Recall the story. Put the correct activities in order and write the letters.

a | b | c

d | e | f

c ⟶ a ⟶ e ⟶ f

2 If you were a friend of Ethan and Ivan, would you like to spend your summer holidays at their grandparents' place in the countryside? Discuss with your friend.

在那儿，我可以吃水果。

在那儿，我可以吃……

我可以看动物。

我可以……

我想去他们的爷爷奶奶家，因为我喜欢大自然／……

城市里有很多商店，我喜欢买玩具。

城市里有很多商店，我喜欢……

我不想去那里，因为城市里更方便。

我可以去公园。

我可以去……

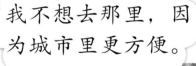

参考表达见上方。

New words

延伸活动：
学生结合本课生词和已学单词，以玲玲的角度谈论自己的暑假计划。
如：暑假来了，我想出去玩，希望天气别太热。星期一，我想先骑马，
然后带布朗尼去玩，我希望我的朋友也可以来一起玩。

1 Learn the new words.

2 Work with your friend. Say the words in the pictures and ask your friend to point to them.

听听说说 Listen and say

03 **1** Listen and circle the correct pictures.

1 上午先去做什么？

2 在公园里可以做什么？

3 明天几点要坐车回家？

04 **2** Look at the pictures. Listen to the story an

小朋友，你们好！这里有很多好玩的活动。我带你们看看。

浩浩，前面有河！

知道了！跳、跳、跳！

第一题录音稿：

小朋友你们好！今天是暑假旅行的最后一天。我们上午先去骑马，然后去饭馆吃饭。下午，我们去公园。大家可以打网球和玩游戏，但是别去河里游泳或者捉鱼。晚上七点，大家一起看电影。八点半回房间。请大家别太晚睡觉，因为明天早上八点要坐车回家。希望你们喜欢今天的活动！

say.

浩浩，你打网球吗？

我先骑马，然后打网球。

这里真好玩，我不想回家了！

我们都不想回家了！

3 Look at the photos and talk to your friend. 参考表达见下方。

1

你想去哪里？

我想先……，然后……

我想先去超市，然后回家。

2

她要买…… 她要买什么？

……先……，然后……

她要先买床，然后买书架。

3

它要……

它要做什么？

它要先玩球，然后睡觉。

第二题参考问题和答案：
1 Where are the children? (They are in a science museum.)
2 Do you like visiting science museums? Why or why not? (Yes, because I am interested in science and technology./No, because I do not like science.)

13

Task

Look at the flyer for a class outing. Think of other activities and design a flyer of your own. Then talk about it with your friend. 参考表达见下方。

四月十八日，我们去公园玩。上午，我们先画画，然后吃饭。下午，……

下午，我们先骑自行车，然后玩球。
真希望天天都来公园玩！

Game

提醒学生有的词可以直接用，如"骑马"和"唱歌"；有的词需要再补充一个动词与之搭配，才能够表示动作，如"饭（吃饭）"和"网球（打网球）"。

Choose two words, make a sentence and ask your friends to do the actions.

我们先骑马，然后回家吃饭。

Chant

延伸活动：
将儿歌第3至6行中的活动换成其他活动，自编新儿歌。活动参考：踢足球、画画、看书、做蛋糕、学汉语、去动物园、打篮球、跑步、游泳、打功夫、上网、玩电脑、弹钢琴。

05 **Listen and say.**

暑假来了，暑假来了，
从早到晚活动多。
星期一，先骑马，
然后打网球。
星期二，你唱歌，
我们来跳舞。
体育馆里做运动，
电影院里看电影。
暑假生活真快乐，
希望天天是暑假！

生活用语 Daily expressions

好玩儿！
This is fun!

好听！
This (The music) is good!

写一写 Write

1 Trace and write the characters.

丿 夕 夕 夕 夕 夗 然 然 然 然 然 然

一 丆 厂 厈 后 后

然	后	然	后
然	后		

丨 冂 冂 回 回 回

丶 丶 宀 宀 宀 宇 家 家 家 家

回	家	回	家
回	家		

2 Write and say.

放学了，我想先去图书馆，＿然后＿和妹妹一起＿回家＿。

3 Fill in the blanks with the correct words. Colour the drums using the same colours.

然后
蓝色

回家
绿色

打球
粉色

时间
黄色

你星期六有 <u>时间</u> 吗？

星期六上午我和爸爸妈妈要出去。我们先去 打球 ，然后 去爷爷家吃饭。下午三点 回家 。你三点半来我家玩吧。

拼音输入法 Pinyin input

Create a paragraph. Choose appropriate letters for the blue, green and pink blanks and complete the yellow ones using your own ideas. Then type it and read it to your friend.

提醒学生根据空格颜色，在相同颜色的选项中选填。

学生可从选项 a–c 任选一个主题，再根据该主题完成段落余下内容。

a 动物	f 看狮子	k 跑步
b 运动	g 吃糖果	l 和小狗玩
c 吃	h 游泳	m 餐馆
d 打功夫	i 画动物	n 公园
e 吃饼干	j 喝汤	o 动物园

我很喜欢＿＿。星期六，我先＿＿，然后＿＿。星期日，我去了＿＿。在那里，我先＿＿，然后＿＿＿＿

＿＿＿＿＿＿＿＿＿＿＿。

星期日的活动应配合该活动发生的地点，即选项 m–o 之一。

参考答案：

我很喜欢动物。星期六，我先和小狗玩，然后画动物。星期日，我去了动物园。在那里，我先看狮子，然后看老虎。昨天，我吃了动物饼干。动物真可爱！

多元学习 Connections

"老鹰捉小鸡"：所有小鸡搭着前面一位的肩膀（或拉着后衣襟）站在母鸡身后，在母鸡的保护下齐力躲避老鹰。当老鹰捉住所有小鸡时，游戏结束，否则母鸡获胜。"跳房子"：其中一种玩法是画一组方格，以数字标明顺序，然后将石子丢入某一格，并往返跳格子。去的途中要避开有石子的一格，回来时则将石子捡起。如果顺利跳完，则这一轮视为成功。"七巧板"：拼摆出的图形需由全部七块板组成，而且板与板之间要有连接。

1 Learn about some traditional Chinese games.

别捉我！

我开始捉人了。

Hawk-and-chicks:
A 'hawk' tries to catch the 'chicks', while a 'hen' protects her children who line up behind her.

一、二、三,
向前跳！

这个飞机颜色真多，真好看！

Hopscotch: Draw squares on the ground, throw a stone into a square, and then hop and jump along the squares to get the stone.

Tangram: A square cut into seven pieces. The pieces can be used to form different shapes.

延伸活动：
在课后与学生玩"老鹰捉小鸡"和"跳房子"的游戏。

2 Make your own tangram. Cut a piece of cardboard into seven pieces. Form different shapes and show them to your friend. Whose shapes are more interesting?

我先骑马，然后坐船。

 →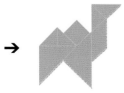

Project

1 Do you like watching films? Have you ever wondered how a film works? Go behind the scenes to see what makes the magic happen.

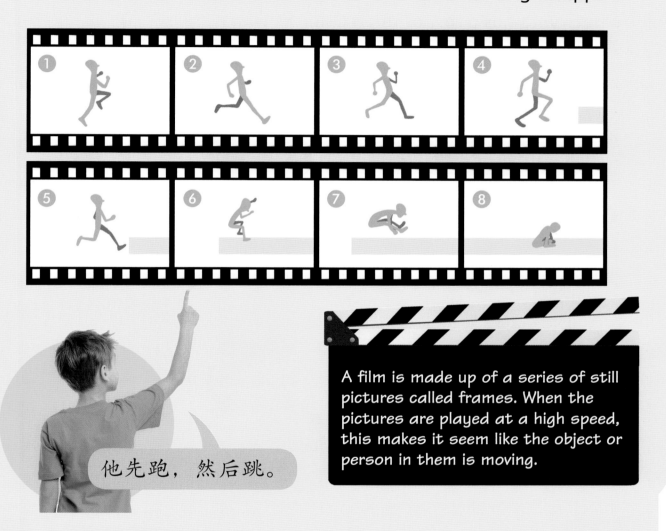

他先跑，然后跳。

A film is made up of a series of still pictures called frames. When the pictures are played at a high speed, this makes it seem like the object or person in them is moving.

2 Use what you have just learnt to create a flip book. Show it to your friend.

他先走，然后跑。

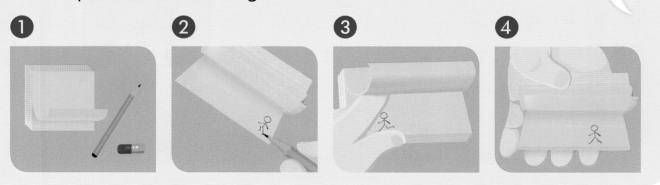

告诉学生，画的张数越多，每两张图之间动作的差别越细微，最终手翻的动画效果会越流畅。

温习 Checkpoint

游戏方法：
学生两人一组，猜拳决定游戏先后次序和"O""X"的使用，然后每人轮流选择一格作答。只有答对题目才能在对应方格画上"O"或"X"。最先在横、竖或斜线方向画满三个"O"或"X"的学生胜出。

1 Play noughts and crosses with your friend. Complete the sentences or write the characters correctly before marking Os or Xs in the squares. The first player who has a row of three Os or Xs wins.

她能 骑马……和 游泳……。

爸爸妈妈…… 带 我们去……超市 买蔬菜和水果。

这只熊在…… 河 里……捉 鱼。

我先吃面包，
然 | 后
写作业。

昨天爸爸在北京工作，今天他
回 | 家 了！

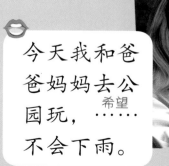

今天我和爸爸妈妈去公园玩，…… 希望 不会下雨。

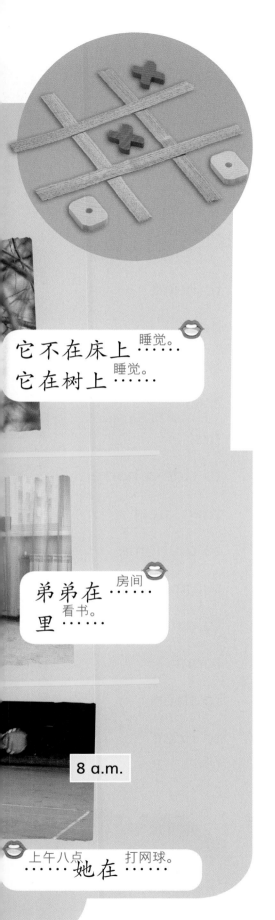

它不在床上睡觉……
它在树上睡觉……

弟弟在房间里……看书。

8 a.m.

……她在打网球上午八点……

2 Work with your friend. Colour the stars and the chillies.

Words and sentences	说	读	写
带	☆	☆	🌶
床	☆	☆	🌶
网球	☆	☆	🌶
河	☆	☆	🌶
先	☆	☆	🌶
骑马	☆	☆	🌶
然后	☆	☆	☆
回家	☆	☆	☆
暑假	☆	🌶	🌶
捉	☆	🌶	🌶
房间	☆	🌶	🌶
睡觉	☆	🌶	🌶
希望	☆	🌶	🌶
第二天，他们先去骑马，然后去爬山。	☆	🌶	🌶

Talk about leisure activities	☆

3 What does your teacher say?

评核建议：

根据学生课堂表现，分别给予"太棒了！(Excellent!)"、"不错！(Good!)"或"继续努力！(Work harder!)"的评价，再让学生圈出左侧对应的表情，以记录自己的学习情况。

分享 Sharing

延伸活动：
1 学生用手遮盖英文，读中文单词，并思考单词意思；
2 学生用手遮盖中文单词，看着英文说出对应的中文单词；
3 学生四人一组，尽量运用中文单词分角色复述故事。

Words I remember

带	dài	to bring
床	chuáng	bed
网球	wǎng qiú	tennis, tennis ball
河	hé	river
先	xiān	first
骑马	qí mǎ	to ride a horse
然后	rán hòu	then, next
回家	huí jiā	to go home
暑假	shǔ jià	summer holidays
捉	zhuō	to catch
房间	fáng jiān	room
睡觉	shuì jiào	to sleep
希望	xī wàng	to hope

Other words

躺	tǎng	to lie
起来	qǐ lái	to get up
赶快	gǎn kuài	immediately
好玩	hǎo wán	fun
爬山	pá shān	to climb a hill/mountain
开心	kāi xīn	happy
离开	lí kāi	to leave
时候	shí hòu	time, moment

OXFORD
UNIVERSITY PRESS

Oxford University Press is a department of the University of Oxford.
It furthers the University's objective of excellence in research, scholarship,
and education by publishing worldwide. Oxford is a registered trade mark of
Oxford University Press in the UK and in certain other countries

Published in Hong Kong by
Oxford University Press (China) Limited
39th Floor, One Kowloon, 1 Wang Yuen Street, Kowloon Bay,
Hong Kong

Illustrated by Anne Lee, Emily Chan, KY Chan and Wildman

Photographs for reproduction permitted by Dreamstime.com

China National Publications Import & Export (Group) Corporation is an authorized distributor of
Oxford Elementary Chinese.

Please contact content@cnpiec.com.cn or 86-10-65856782

ISBN: 978-0-19-082313-9

10 9 8 7 6 5 4 3 2

Teacher's Edition
ISBN: 978-0-19-082325-2

10 9 8 7 6 5 4 3 2